WOUND SCARS

WOUND SCARS

ALDIVAN TORRES

Canary Of Joy

Contents

1 "Wound Scars"   1

I

"Wound Scars"

Aldivan Teixeira Torres
Wound Scars

Author: Aldivan Teixeira Torres
@2018-Aldivan Teixeira Torres
All the rights reserved
Aldivan Teixeira Torres
Translator: Jose Osorio

This book, including all its parts, is protected by copyright and don't can to be reproduced without Autor's permission, resold or transferred.

Short Biography: Aldivan Teixeira Torres, was born in Arcoverde, created the series "The Seer", the series sons of the light, poetry and screenplays. His literary career started at the end of 2011 with the publication of his first romance work Opposing forces – the mystery of the cave. For whatever reason, he stopped writing only resuming his career in the second half of 2013. Since then, he never stopped. He hopes that his writing will contribute to the Pernambuco and Brazilian culture, arousing the pleasure of reading in those that do not yet have the habit. His motto is "For literature, equality, fraternity, justice, dignity and the human being honor forever".

SUMMARY

Dedications and Acknowledgments

I dedicate this work to all the people who live life in the best way possible. We all suffer with misfortunes, we fall into suffering, we sin, we fight, we give up or we persist. What is different from one to the other is the way we face it. Life must be lived in any way and since we are in this ship called Earth let's change this moment into a period of reflection, pleasure and overcoming. We must overcome our "Wound scars" which are inevitable.

I give thanks to my spiritual father, my family, my friends, work colleagues, acquaintances, relatives, neighbors, compatriots, to my loved readers and to all who have encouraged reading. Let's make country of carnival and football also the country of culture. Let's value the Brazilian literature, with so much hidden talent out there.

"Free me, oh God, quick, Lord, help me! Let those who try to take my life be ashamed and confounded. Let those who crave for my misfortune, retreat and be stunned. Retreat, cover in shame those who say: Ah! Ah! Let all those who search for you to rejoice and be happy; and those who love your salvation repeat incessantly: God is great! As for me, poor and indigent, come quickly, oh God! You are my support, my savior, Lord, do not delay!

(Psalm 70(69)

Introduction

"Wound scars" is a book intended for all mortals. Through the line of time and the adventure, it is possible to see yourself facing the difficulties of each character and through the lessons learnt, to gain a new direction in life.

At the end, we hope that there will be reflection and a true resumption of life. For we must not allow the "Scars" and our own fear to take control of the reins of our existence, but to have a pro-active attitude in life. Enjoy the reading and I sincerely hope that you will greatly benefit from it.

Chapter 1 – The Return

The seer is back. After a long and intense journey beside the archangels, Renato and thirteen incredible persons, he is back home again. Little by little, he is assuming the normal routine: The job at the public services, the constant trips back and forwards to the city, the contact with the family, with the neighbors and with the readers, his writing side which needs dedication, publicizing, persistence and great faith. Finally, he is completely immersed in his "I am" relentless day to day. However, he is conscious that he can go further and takes the decision of not stopping.

In the day to day of life something important happens. Let me share it with you:

"The seer was in Arcoverde, near the business district when he was briefly approached by a man apparently in distress. He said that he lived in Sertania and that his mother gravely ill at the city's regional hospital. He mentioned that he did not have any money neither to take care of her nor even to ask for help from his relatives at home. He begged in the name of God for help, for he didn't have hope or salvation.

Feeling sorry for the distressed man and touched deep down in his soul, for the man's situation, Aldivan decided to help. Took a few notes from his wallet and gave them to him, saying: **Go and help your mother, buy some food and go home.** *Smiling, the man put the money away, not even saying thank you and disappeared in the middle of the crowd. He stayed there alone".*

The funniest thing is what happened next. After his deed of kindness, he continued walking along the town's main avenue, Colonel Antonio Japiassu, and within five minutes something spectacular happened to him. In the middle of the lane, there were his two great friends and masters of the previous adventure of the series "Sons of the Light". They were carrying two backpacks and eating a sandwich which they have bought at the corner shop. Getting closer and before could spring a surprise he was noticed. Greetings and hugging followed. The happiness of the reunion is all round. Inevitably, the conversation starts:

"Emmanuel, Messias, how good to see you. How long has it been? How are you? (Asked Divine)

"I am well, master. Everything as usual. (Emmanuel)

"Yes, and how did you feel helping that man? (Messias)

"I felt good. Helping others rouse in us our best feelings. Charity is a way of redeeming the faults of the human being. (Taught the Son of God).

"I know, I know. And in the case that you may have been tricked, do you feel angry with that man? (Messias)

"I didn't even think about that possibility. What is important is my deed. Whether he lied or not, it is own responsibility. Many people do not help for fear. Fear, many times also makes them give up, isolate themselves, feeling incapable. I, however, will say to you: Help and love your neighbor, for, that attitude may change the life of many people. (The seer)

"It is what I wanted to hear, master. I thank the father for having put you in our way. Your light gives us a full life and I think that the world also deserves being illuminated by that light. (Messias Escapuleto)

"I agree with you. Since I have saved you from that fatal tragedy, I understood its importance. Man, I was really missing you. (Emmanuel Melkin Escapuleto)

"I was also missing you. You were angels that entered my life and had transformed it. What are you doing here in the city? (Aldivan)

"We are on our way to the bus station. One of our best friends is in trouble and we are going to try to help him rebuild. (Messias)

"Do you want to join us, son of God? Who knows if with your presence he will not feel better? (Emmanuel)

"Where are going to? How long? (The son of God)

"We are going to Buíque. (Messias)

"For an indeterminate time. (Added Emmanuel)

"Oh, yes. I love Buíque. Just wait a moment. (Aldivan)

Aldivan moves a little away from his companions, ruffle his clothes, his hair, the sun glasses and talks on the cell phone. He asks his boss for permission to stay away from work for some time, alleging some grave danger. Touched, the boss gives his permission. Afterwards, he makes a call to his family and inform them of a work trip as writer. He stresses that he will be away for an indeterminate time. Despite the shock his family accepts. Right. Now he is free to accomplish his mission, to help a person to re-establish his deepest dreams. "The seer" was again in action, in this case in the series "Sons of light" with his companions of Italian stock Emanuel and Messias.

With the call finished, he returns to his friends and they all depart to the mentioned destination. The three of them walk along the length of the avenue, turn the corner, pass the cathedral of deliverance, a supermarket, pass in front of the city's business district and turn another corner. The official bus station place of Arcoverde, is about one hundred meters ahead, the Brazilian backwoods capital.

Our esteemed friends make this last part of the route with enthusiasm and dedication. At this precise moment, the predominant feeling is one of anxiety, nervousness, desire for new adventures, fear of the unknown and the unpredictable. As by magic, they were going to leave the sameness of their routine, that for the son of God, consisted actually of travelling from work-home and for the others the placid life in Jeritacó, a village lost in the northeast backwoods, characterized by a constant drought and forgotten by most of the authorities.

Arriving at the destination, they go to Buíque's station, and as this locality is nearby and its industry and commerce are linked to the Arcoverde's hub, the movement of people is constant at any time. Thus, they don't have to wait long before the vehicle (A silver beast of twelve seats) parks up.

Leaving the bus stop, the vehicle quickly reaches the town center, Saint Christopher and other neighborhoods. Soon after they reach, he third on-off ramp of the city, cross the BR 232 highway and on the other side they reach the state highway PE 270. Travelling along the new road, they take advantage of the trip to relax and reflect about the last events.

From the seer's side, there was a very clear adventure where he will gather the apostles and will discover a great part of the state counties. He will teach about his Father and how to awaken internal "I am" of each of them. From the sons of light's side, Messias Escapuleto, the father, and Emanuel Melkin Escapuleto- the son- were planning all this time a reunion with theirs loved master, but that he didn't even suspect. As the old saying goes, everything in its time.

Now there they were, the three reunited, looking forward to meet with somebody in need of help. In the son of God's case, he has already had this attitude with numerous persons: Christine, Claudio, Clodoaldo, Phillipe Andrews, the farmer who was the virgin Mary, the little humble girl that he had known at the social care, the beggar and many more. Each one of them had a tragic story and was comforted in his arms. He would always repeat this gesture.

This was the marvelous son of God, a nice guy, humble, dignified, patient, believer, able, a visionary with pre-concepts or discriminations. Together with their adventure companions, the sons of light, they hoped to transform many lives.

In this assurance, they continue to advance on the highway PE 270. They pass through places, villages, going through the surrounding immense grey area. Buíque, apart from being an enormous county was an area of many natural wonders.

Everything there was perfect for the beginning of a new adventure. This new stage certainly would bring new surprises that Emanuel and Messias intended to preserve in time. Let's go forward.

A while later, the journey is finished and straight away at the beginning of the urban perimeter they ask to stop. They climb down from the vehicle, pay the fares and walk a few meters in the quiet city. They stop in front of the door of the third house on the righthand side of the place first street. A house of contemporary style, of medium size, measuring 12x5 meters, the entrance door on righthand side and the window on the left side, a sitting room, two bedrooms, communal bathroom, a kitchen were the house compartments and a small wall.

Softly, they knock at the door and listening to the approaching sound of steps they wait a while. Immediately, the door is opened and inside appears a thin man, about forty years of age, tall, black hair, eyes light brown color, features of average beauty with a low nose, normal eyebrows, medium size mouth, protruding ears, lean and narrow waist, hairy, thin arms and legs. With a smiling face, he greets his acquaintances and faces the seer with a suspicious look, starting the conversation:

"Welcome. Who is the young man with you?"

"This is our adventure companion, Aldivan Teixeira Torres, author re-known worldwide. (Emanuel explained)

"Tadeu, he is also our "Master of the light". (Messias)

"Caramba! A writer and master. Congratulations. (Tadeu Barbosa)

"Thank you. It is a great mission that I must achieve with your collaboration. (The seer)

"Very well, come in and make yourselves at home. (Tadeu)

Accepting the invitation, the three went in the humble residence accompanied by the host. In the living room, which is the first room, they sat on a five-seat couch making themselves comfortable. Above the couch, is a picture of an ewe. On the righthand side, there is a simple metal shelf where there is a TV and a medium size battery radio. A relaxed conversation develops between them.

"How good that you have arrived. My life fell into a tedious routine from which I cannot escape. (Tadeu)

"I have received your letter. As soon as I read it, I spoke to my son and together we decided to answer you call. That is what friends are for. (Messias Escapuleto)

"Yes. We are always at your service. (Emanuel)

"I am here to get to know you and help you too. (Son of God)

"I thank the three of you. How is work and personal life? (Tadeu)

"At the moment, I live on my pension and stay more at home. (Messias)

"I work in the fields and other small jobs. With the money, I help at home and go out at the weekends. I am reasonably well. (Emanuel Melkin Escapuleto)

"I have my official job as public servant and as writer. Both give me pleasure. In my personal life, I am still not completely accomplished. (The seer)

"You are very well. In my life, nothing is practically left. As time went by, I have only accumulated misfortunes. They are "Wound scars" that settle in and don't want ever to get out. (He confessed)

"For that reason, we brought the son of God with us. He is the only being able to change your situation. (Messias)

"How? (Tadeu)

"Explain to him, master. (Emanuel)

"I am what I am. Through his greatness, my father has nominated me to help the poor sinners. I can see, feel and understand your problems and help change your future. Believing is enough. (Aldivan)

Tadeu was dumbfounded. How can you change my future? As time went by, with the sequence of constant failures he had lost completely his faith in God and people. However, there was a contradiction. He absolutely trusted his friends Emanuel and Messias and if they went through the trouble of bringing that man to his presence there must be a true and strong reason to do so. Who knows whether a great miracle couldn't be possible or not?

"I am going to give you one chance. What is the next step? (Tadeu)

"To meet with god. Do know Catimbau? (Aldivan)

"I know the village, but I never went to the park. (Informed Tadeu)

"Very well. Catimbau is the perfect place for my plans. (Aldivan)

"Excellent idea, master. (Messias)

"We are right behind you. (Emanuel) "Very good. Let's get the backpacks ready. We will leave in the afternoon. Tadeu, I am going to need some of your clothes. (Aldivan)

"No problem. There are enough clothes for everybody. (Tadeu)

"Excellent. Let's go! (The seer)

From the room where they were they went to the master bedroom and together they separate the basic needed to spend a short stay. They choose clothes, personal things, an inflatable tent, books, a radio, sun screen, a watch and food to cook and already made. After finishing this stage, they went to prepare lunch in the kitchenette. In there, they share the duties: Whilst Aldivan and Tadeu prepare the ingredients, Messias and Emanuel are given the task of cooking. In this way, each one directly participates in the preparation of the meal.

Two hours later, everything is ready. They sit down at the small table and help themselves. While eating, they alternate between silence and short conversation. Everything is very pleasant and inviting between them, opening news perspectives for the hearts of the foursome.

Thirty minutes later, they finish the meal. After, they take care of their physiologic needs as a preventive measure and go to care of the last details of the trip. With everything ready, they go to the exit and once outside they lock the house. Towards new challenges!

They walk a few hundred meters and crossing the center, they stop at the main square. Tadeu Barbosa knows the town very well and then he contacts a well-known and trusted taxi driver who have stopped his Fiat Uno car on the righthand side of the square.

"Mr. Fabricio Toledo, can you take us to Catimbau? (Tadeu)

"Of course, brother. You and these three men? (Fabricio)

"Yes, they are my friends Aldivan, Emanuel and Messias. (Tadeu)

"Pleased to meet you. I am available to take you for fifty dollars. Is it alright? (Fabricio)

"It is alright with me. What do you think, my friends? (Tadeu)

"It is fine with me, as well. (The seer)

"Excellent. (Messias)

"Let's go, then! (Emanuel Melkin Escapuleto)

One after the other they get in the car. After, the driver also gets in and starts the trip. Catimbau was awaiting them certainly with great surprises. Let's go together, readers!

Chapter 2- Towards Catimbau

We begin the journey which promises plenty of emotions. Leaving the tarred road, they take a detour on a dirt road going straight ahead. The state of the way is deplorable causing numerous bumps in the car. Apart from that, the sensation is terrific: The air is pure, the mountains, the farms, the rocks and the backwoods are elements that make the place unique. Without a doubt, one of the most beautiful places in the world.

At that precise moment, our friends' mental state was oscillating from excitement to complete nervousness. What is the son of God preparing for them? What did he have in mind with that trip to Catimbau? The mystery behind all this seemed immense. However, they did not have the courage of confronting him there. They preferred to the live the magic of every moment as if it was the last one and time itself would present them with necessary answers. So, they hoped.

In a constant rhythm, they advance even in the face of great difficulties. Half way, they ask the driver to stop and take some photos of the landscape. The objective was to keep memories and document them, to show the family and probable children, grandchildren and great grandchildren. In the end, they would be proud of saying: I was briefly here.

Ten minutes later, they return to the car and restart the journey. The driver increases the speed, for the road becomes better. The last six kilometers were covered in ten minutes. They arrived at Catimbau; a rustic place lost in the Brazil's wild immensity. The taxi driver drops our friends at the local guides association, where they contract one of them to guide them to the park. We take leave of Fabricio, keeping his phone number to be contacted later.

Once a guide was contracted, and they plan the itinerary and a small truck is rented to take them to a point near the park. Everything is ready. The guide introduces himself as Paulo Lacerda, who also acts as driver, and with the help of the vehicle they surmount the climb's difficulties. At this moment, the adrenalin is pumping strongly, leaving the tourists in awe even before reaching the ecologic sanctuary.

Arriving at the furthest point the vehicle can reach, they alight and begin the itinerary on foot. They follow a narrow path, full of obstacles to be faced: difficult climbs and descents, thorns and dangerous scabs in that landscape called "plateau".

After walking for about two hours, they stop and they start clear the terrain in a clearing they have found. They pitch the tent and rest for a while. A while later, they went to look for firewood in the forest and when they found some, they return and lit a fire. They begin to prepare a simple dinner, onion soup. Directly or indirectly, everybody contributes to the harmonious atmosphere and cooking dinner. When the food is ready, they feed themselves there in the forest without any comfort. It is the price to pay for daring so much. However, nobody complained. Catimbau served a release valve to their personal frustrations, and the break, changed the monotonous routine of most of them. To be there, in the middle of the forest, beside mother nature was better than win a prize. It was a privilege for only a few.

Once dinner is finished, the seer stands up in front of them and starts talking:

"My dear friends, from my life experience, I selected a few important points for discussion at this sanctuary. I have brought you here exactly in view to absorb the so needed knowledge. Everything all right?

"Everything. My experience in life has brought me only chaos. So, it is good to learn. (Tadeu Barbosa)

"Last time, I was the master but now the role is yours. Be at ease. (Messias)

"You are the light's master. You have got all the attributes to teach. (Emanuel)

"I am a stranger in the nest, but I will pay attention to your teachings. (Paulo Lacerda) "Thank you all. The theme that I want to discuss concerns the family basis. I was born to a humble family, son of farmers and because they were raised in the decade (in the frontier of the Brazilian northeast), they received a rigid upbringing from their parents, including frequent beatings, child labor, poverty and discrimination. They have absorbed these values and acted in same way with me, what caused great frustration, sadness, distance and incomprehension. I don't find fair this kind of treatment and I have promised myself that I would not perpetuate it in the case I would get married. How was your experience and what do you think about it? (The seer)

"I am a native of Sicily's region, in Italy, and in my time, the family behavior was similar to the one you have just described. We were seven siblings and food were scarce. My parents were absent and that caused various twists. Often, the older ones took advantage of the weakness of the younger ones (Hitting them) and our parents didn't even know or pretended that they did not know. Arriving in Brazil, each one went their own way, my grandparents and my parents died, and we built our own families. Thus, we have prioritized justice, equality and peace among the family members. (Related Messias Escapuleto)

"Thank God, I and my father are happy in our family unit. As he mentioned, in his time, things had a different connotation. However, even nowadays, there are evidence of problematic families. (Emanuel Melkin Escapuleto)

"My father was very strict. I had to start working early and I couldn't study. I grew without any education eating wood, stone, dust and dragging snakes by the feet. So be happy my friend for the opportunity of having had an education and being the man that you are today. (Observed Paulo Lacerda)

"Paulo is right, Aldivan. My life was much more complicated than yours and even so I survived. So, you should feel blessed. (Tadeu Barbosa)

"I understand you all and I understand myself. Family is the first community in which we participate and in it we learn how to share, to dialogue, to interact with strangers. Nothing occurs without suffering, for there isn't a perfect family. What I want to pass to you and to the public, is that have the right to choose. We are not our parents nor we should follow their example in everything for they imperfect beings. The one who we must imitate is called Yahweh and his son Jesus Christ who have left their commandments on Earth. Through them, we can reach perfection and obtain the desired results in every field. Blessed be our father! (Aldivan)

"Amen! (The others)

"Let's us now talk about modern problems. To you, what is family nowadays and what is its importance according to your experiences? (Aldivan)

"To compare the family of the present with the one of the pasts it is an impossible task. In the past, children respected and feared their parents more. Nowadays, progress has destroyed the concept of family. (Messias Escapuleto)

"There are also differences between the rural family and city family, besides the diverse social strata. (Observed Emanuel)

"My family is like any other, with problems, misunderstandings and agreements. To be able to handle this it is typical of a conscious citizen of the state of the democratic right. Thank God that I have not followed my parents' way and nowadays my children can study. (Paulo Lacerda)

"I don't want to go into that. It is a "Wound scar" that still hurts a lot. (Tadeu Barbosa)

"Why my friend? May I help you? (Seer)

"At this moment, I don't want to talk about it. I want to know you better and yes, maybe you can help me. (Tadeu)

"I fully understand you. No problem, I will wait for the right time. (Seer)

"Thank you very much. (Tadeu)

"Don't mention it. Very well. End of the talk. Let's enjoy the rest of the evening. (The seer)

"OK. (The others)

The night progresses and the cold increases ever more. The scouts gather round the fire to get warm and to talk a bit more. There, in that piece of ground, each one takes advantage of his individuality to absorb the teachings of the mother earth and the son of God. The gravest case was Tadeu's who was carrying deep" Wound scars", which have not healed yet, but he was not the exception. Messias Escapuleto, Emanuel Melkin Escapuleto, Paulo Lacerda and even the master of light himself have all suffered. The difference between them was that the latter, was capable of overcoming it, and go forward with his life. "The seer" was a rare case prepared to teach and to listen to his superiors, subordinates and friends. This was a very important lesson for mankind in general.

Besides the learning and the adventure, the trip was a great opportunity of freedom from life's monotony. How many times haven't we got bored or get into a deep depression for the simple fact of a routine repetition? Whenever we reach this point, the best thing to do is to change drastically: Talk, walk, learn new things, watch TV, go to the cinema, read a book, are just a few things we can do to change our routine. Our brain demands a constant fluctuation between the various pleasurable activities in life. We cannot stop.

Aware of this, they try to enjoy the rest of the evening in the best way possible. Later, they plan a schedule of turns to look out for wild animals. It works in the following manner: One stays on the lookout for a certain time, while the others sleep. After, they take it in turns.

Thus, it was made. From twenty-two hours (22H00), four goes to sleep and one stays on guard. Two hours later, is the turn of the next one and so on. The only one to be excused of this task is the group leader. For obvious reasons, he needs total rest and concentration to face the following days in the forest. So, the night and dawn have passed and finally it is early morning.

Chapter 3- Trail of the stone of the dog and Towers

Very early, our ecologic tourists wake up. They get up, stretch and come out of the tent. The next step, is to make a fire and prepare breakfast. What is available to eat are some sweet potatoes well preserved and cooked to the exact point of being savored. To go with, they also make a pot of traditional coffee.

When everything is ready, they start to eat and the sun comes out very strong. The day was perfect for another great adventure and respective discoveries by our esteemed personalities. However, the doubts and worries continue to persist and were hammering their minds. What did the son of God really have in mind when bringing them to that end of the world?

Whatever it was, the others trusted entirely his wisdom, love and dedication. Certainly, there would be good news. While the future was not yet planned, they took advantage to interact during twenty minutes of breakfast and at the end, they begin to prepare for the day's journey.

From the actual trail, they would follow to the area that includes the trail of the stone of the dog, the Lapiás and the trail of the Towers.

In view of that, they unpitched the tent, adjust the backpacks, tide up and start walking led by the guide. On a narrow trail and of difficult access they move away from plateau's area going ahead and also sideways, after short period of time, to the area regarding the trail of the stone of the dogs.

Following the respective trail, overcoming the forest natural obstacles and being witnesses to the beautiful landscape incrusted in the mountain, they arrive at the first touristic spot. It concerns of a medium size stony hill, surrounded by a caatinga. They tourists take photos of this important wild symbol, that in a distant past witnessed the development of the native population, the Indians. It was a time of fighting, discoveries, masks and cruelty.

Five minutes later, they go ahead in search of another spot to take they breath away. Going forward through unknown landscapes at a moderate pace, they continue motivated and in good spirits. In truth, the seer had an excellent idea bringing them there. The next feature of the journey is a stony hill, a set of rocky points well spread in the middle of the nature. In relation to the previous spot, they were on west side facing a stony hill, on the righthand side the immense greenery and on the left-hand side the mountain itself. They take advantage of the place to drink and have a short rest from the exhaustive walk. However, there was much to be discovered.

Thinking of that, a short while later, they return to the speedy walk that they planned earlier. The trail took them to another important spot: An interesting geologic formation, well worked by nature, high, slippery, deformed and with vestiges of rock paintings. It was one of the few monuments of that park preserving these landmarks of the ancient civilization. In front of it, our friends take photos appreciating its peculiar beauty. How marvelous was the northern landscape! The astonishment is so great they cannot believe that they are there, savoring this striking moment capable of causing to reflect and of healing the worst maladies. Blessed be the son of God!

Inspired by everything they have seen so far, they restart the journey, with more conviction, happy and willing. The walk really was having effect on their suffering souls. To whom do they owe it to? In first place, to God, the son and to fate that had given a little help. Everything was going little by little towards the solution of their problems.

Walking further into the woods, the guide takes them to a peculiar place: The group finds itself on the edge of the canyon and some more courageous sit at the edge challenging the height.

If by accidental chance they slip, nothing would remain from their mortal bodies, such was the place's height. Incredible work of nature. The exchange impressions in between themselves, take more photos, they rest a little on the rocky formation and study the environment. The vegetation is typical of the caatinga presenting great variety of specimens with bromeliads and cacti in abundance. As for the fauna, more than one hundred fifty species are known, as an example the goldfinch, the Maria-Macambira, the little woodpecker, the rock lizard and the Kluge lizard among others.

After twenty minutes, they say goodbye to this landscape and carry on in search of the last attraction of the day. Meandering by the trail, our friends face the scolding sun, the dust, the sharp stones, the painful thorns, the tiredness, and the constant danger of meeting venomous or wild animals. In the meantime, the walk was worth the pain.

A little further on, they are faced with the day's last great landscape: A harmonious and homogenic set of natural faults spread along the plain immediately below the mountain where they stood. Lined up, the hills resembled chess pieces on the great board that is the planet Earth. The players would be God and fate and the other pieces the humans in their majority perverts. Just like in the game, life would progress in accordance with the moves of those responsible, and as they were wise everything was going to be right in the end. It was what everybody expected.

It was eleven o'clock in the morning and by mutual consent, the group decide to make camp there, on that same place looking onto the natural faults. With everybody's help, they pitch the tent, look for firewood in the woods and lit a small fire.

The objective was to prepare everybody's lunch. As last time, everyone co-operated and one and half hour later the grub was ready. They begin to help themselves and to savor the rice and the "drover" beans. In this time interval, for about thirty minutes, moments of silence alternate with exchange of important information between them. At the end of this of time, they take care of the finalization of the lunch, wash the dishes and put out the fire. Soon after, they get together in a circle and "The master of the light" stood up and starts talking:

"My friends and brothers I want to tell you something. I want to talk about the modern society full of rules, impositions and moral concepts. Firstly, how is your relationship with external environment, the so-called contemporary society?

"I have lived two types of situations: One more backward where everything was subject of scandal and the actual more liberal in every sense. However, there were always be rules to follow. (Stated Messias)

"I think that there is a dichotomy involved in all of that. We have an elite society that dictates all the rules and a lower class that is submissive to it. There is also a society layered by ethnicity, religion and sexual choice. (Emanuel Melkin Escapuleto opined)

"I would also include in that classification the regional stratification. The reality of the North and the Northeast is completely different of the other regions, meaning, the rules also change a little. Here, we don't have many options. (Paulo Lacerda)

"In my humble opinion, the society is in decadence, for it is not able to safeguard the rights of the less fortunate. What we see is exacerbated violence and lack of respect. I have long ago stopped believing in the power of the society. (Tadeu Barbosa)

"I agree with all of you. In fact, the human society has got many distortions in its several spheres. My advice is that you follow your own values even if they contradict these blessed rules. Yahweh, our father, has created us with our own personality and we must play the principal role on the stage of this theatre that is life. Let's us be authentic! (The seer)

"Master, what do you say about the society's contempt and spite for minorities? (Enquired Emanuel)

"It is a very grave matter. Thinking about it, I have written a book "I am", the fifth in the "The seer" series where I give a shout of freedom and confront that same society. In the book, I accept as criminal apostles, depressive, corrupt, disabled, an abortionist, scientists and even a priest. Thus, I demonstrate that I and my Father do not have pre-concepts and our kingdom is open for everybody. It is only enough a sincere change of attitude, to give his cross to me, to embrace the cause of goodness and believe in our name. "I am" is not a human being, it is a perfect being and unlike the society that only judges, believes in you. (Aldivan, the son of God)

"Blessed be the master. We made the right choice in bringing you here. Soon, our friend Tadeu will be cured of "Wound scars". (Emanuel)

"I believe so. Every moment I am more surprised about this uncommon man. The confidence is being consolidated little by little. (Tadeu Barbosa)

"Thank you. (The son of God)

"Talking about that, son of God, I believe that pre-conception and pride are very difficult to combat. It is almost impossible having a realistic view. (Messias)

"I am conscious of that, Messias. But for that, at the end of time, there is the separation of good and bad ones: "I will gather the wheat in my silo and I will throw out the straw in the darkness outside. Those who have ears to listen, ought to listen." (The son of God)

"Aldivan, how about my situation? A simple man, farmer, guide and driver, who has been crucified by life? (Paulo Lacerda)

"My Father knows everything. In due time, you will receive the just reward for your labors and will reach peace, I believe. (Aldivan)

"I, believe! (Paulo)

"Amen! Let's return to our other activities. (The seer)

Obeying the seer's command, the conversation was taken as finished and the silence hovered among them. In the remainder of the afternoon and evening, they conduct several activities: Resting in the tent, walking on the surroundings, listen to music on the battery radio, plan the future, to prepare dinner and when ready (replenish the energies), study the stars and chat in the evening, and sleep. The following day will certainly bring more new events, in that intriguing wild jungle. Good night everyone.

Chapter 4- Trail of the cave

It is early morning in the paradise of Catimbau and the inviting rising sun helps everybody to wake up. One by one, they rise from the hard and dry ground, have a stretch and organize themselves for the task of making breakfast. Emanuel, Messias and Paulo go to fetch firewood from the woods and when they return with it, the cooking is left to the chefs Aldivan Teixeira and Tadeu Barbosa. The two are working together and both are culinary experts. The first one enjoyed cooking whenever he had spare time and the second one was forced, from very early, by the circumstances to look after himself.

As the forest is an inhospitable place and without many options, the day's menu is biscuits and fried eggs. Even so, nobody complains and after it is ready, they share the food between themselves. While they are eating, they happily exchange information with objective of getting closer and increase the bonding between them. Together, they were the group of the "Son of light", also an important series of the son of God.

"Paulo, you that knows the place well, will we have more surprises ahead? (Tadeu Barbosa)

"Of course. Catimbau is a park about Sixty-two thousand and three hundred hectares (62300 ha) in size, incorporating the counties of Buíque, Ibimirim and Tupanatinga. Even I being a guide don't know it entirely. (Paulo)

"Incredible. The seer is a genius for having the idea of bringing us here. Even with such torturous past I am hopeful. (Tadeu Barbosa)

"I have brought you here exactly for that reason. Imagine that the past doesn't exist and that you are being born now. You will be free to dream and will the necessary trust in me, your redemption. (Interned the son of God)

"I am going to try. (Promised Tadeu)

"I am starting to admire you as well. Let's go towards this God's light. (Paulo)

"Me too, I was your master and now I am your servant, for nobody knows everything to the point of not being able to learn and so ignorant that cannot teach. (Messias Escapuleto)

"I saved you, from being run over by a lorry, and now I am being saved by your words. (Emanuel Melkin Escapuleto)

"I thank you all for your kind words. I continue being a young dreamer forever. The difference is that I am assured and decisive where to walk. To those who follow me, I promise a kingdom of pleasure where everybody is equal. My kingdom is a paradise where milk and honey run in abundance. Those who taste my and my father's love will never be thirsty or hungry. It is written that the loyal servants will worship the father and his sons in the Mount Siam. At that time, peace will reign on Earth. (The son of God)

- Let me enter your kingdom, Son of God! I cannot stand my terrible life anymore. Wherever I go I only find curse and bad luck. If were not your visit and this trip I would already be dead. Have pity on me, for the love of God! (Tadeu Barbosa)

"Relax, brother! Do you think I don't suffer too? I also feel in my humanity the human sorrows. I have already faced misery, I have already been rejected and despised by mankind, I have already had important family losses, I have also failed, I was treated unfairly, I have been ignored and have been confused. However, my father always believed me and saved me.

"For the grace I have received, I also will act in the same way with others. I love him as I love myself and this eternal love extend to all of mankind, even if it does not deserve it. It is like that for the love of the Father, without reservations. (The seer)

"I understand you. Forgive me for the unburden. (Tadeu Barbosa)

"Don't worry. Unburdening is good. We are here to support you. (The son of God)

"Thank you. (Tadeu)

"Tadeu, the son of God is absolutely right, we all carry "Wound scars" from our past and some are very troublesome. We must learn to overcome them and Aldivan is the only one that can give us the right elements to achieve it. (Emanuel)

"It is not by chance that he is the master of the light, sent by God to re-establish the contact between God and the lost mankind. Let's have faith! (Messias)

"Yes. I am going to try to persist, brothers! Thank you for your help. (Tadeu Barbosa)

"A very interesting discussion. I am going to take advantage of the trip and learn to control my fears and problems too. (Paulo Lacerda)

"Relax, brother. I am available to help all those in need. Ask and you will be given, knock and it will open, search and you will find. God's Spirit will bless without restrictions for he is Father and not stepfather. (Aldivan)

"Amen! (The others)

Suddenly the conversation stops and they get on with the breakfast. A few minutes later, they have finished and the son of God speaks again, shuffling his hair and unshaved beard. His dirty jeans, his jersey, his blue underpants and his black high boots gave him a more respectable appearance.

"Let's continue our mission. We dismantle the tent and arrange the backpacks to carry on with the walk. Brothers, let's go!

Soon after, his friends and Aldivan himself went to take care of the last details. At that exact moment, harmony reigned among them despite the nervousness, the worries and the uncertainty. What would happen to them? What did The God and his sons intend to do with their lives? The mysterious atmosphere surrounding the master was still great. What they knew about him was that he was a simple young man, farmer from outback of Pernambuco and was transformed by the action of the spirit. His face showed the divine mark of confidence, of kindness, generosity and humanity. Independently of who he really was, he was without any doubt a special being destined to change the life of many people with his name bringing the power and importance of the son of God. Polemics aside, he deserved this title, for his life history had real proof of his actions and together with the father making a great miracle.

With everything ready, they get together and with the help of the guide they depart for one more intriguing adventure: The forbidden cave of Catimbau. From the local where they were- Towers- they look for a nearby trail which would take them to their destiny. With Paulo's experience of the shortcuts in the woods, within half an hour of effort they reach the top of the mountain, separating the actual trail and the one they wanted. From there, according to the information, they would have access to the cave's entrance in less than four hours.

Overcoming the division, they began the descent of the escarpment through an improvised trail, due to the fact that the l was little known and visited. Surrounded by abysms on both sides, our friends strive to avoid slipping down the steep hills. Any slip would be fatal. One, two, three hours and sometime later they can see the cave's entrance. At this moment, the adrenalin and nervousness are at the maximum. They were at the point of facing a very dangerous cave, habitat to about forty species of bats, besides snakes and other venomous animals.

A few steps ahead, they are already facing the dangerous place. At about one hundred meters long, the place imposes itself by the mysticism and darkness. Statics, the son of God and his companions seek courage to enter it.

Even facing a great challenge, our friends are great combatants. Holding hands, they form a line and one by one go into the cave. With the help of a torch, they initially perceive the low ceiling of the cave. They must walk against the rock, because there a great abysm on the side. With the experience and expertise of Paulo Lacerda, they luckily overcome this stage.

In the next section, the cave's ceiling becomes higher and the proximity to the bats, makes the atmosphere heavier. It is necessary to take the outmost care so as not to upset them and cause an accident. The seer takes advantage of this moment to say a prayer in an unknown language what causes a certain peace and tranquility in the others.

They stay at the place for about five minutes more and then make their way back. Carefully, they leave the second section, enter the first one and reach the exit without major problems. Now the little cave will stay behind.

Outside, they camp, pitch the tent, bring firewood from the woods and begin to prepare lunch. Two hours later, everything is ready, they eat and they rest. For the remainder of the afternoon and evening, they plan the next steps prepare dinner and eat, go for walks in the surroundings, admire the starry night and talk for hours on end. The main points of the conversation are described below:

"My friends and brothers, I want to touch on a delicate subject. How do you face the challenges of the daily life? (The seer)

"My challenge is to look after my family and my work. I love these two spheres of action. In my family, I discover the pleasure of being spouse and father, and my work satisfies me besides being my livelihood. Who didn't wish to be always in contact with the wonderful nature? (Paulo Lacerda)

"You are right, colleague, it a blessing to be here beside such special people. I got hope despite my turbulent life up to now. (Tadeu Barbosa)

"My challenge is to have to live with an arid and dry land. In the last few years, it has been a disaster for agriculture. Apart from that I am happy with my son. (Messias Escapuleto)

"Apart from what my father has said, people's prejudice, the lack of work opportunities, the social rules make today's youth life difficult. (Emanuel Melkin Escapuleto)

"I understand all of you. I also have my own difficulties. Life has always challenged me since I was younger: The difficult childhood having gone through hard times, the humiliation caused by those circumstances, my impossible passions, the unemployment and insecurity that dominate for a long time, my dark night of the soul where I forget the good principles. The crucial event was when the angel intervened and saved me from the claws of darkness. From then on, the achievements appeared and my life became much better at the cost of dedication and sweat. All this was possible because I am a cool an optimistic human being who always believes in God and in my project. And you? Do you persist with your dreams or do you give up? (The son of God)

"Life never gave me a chance of surviving. So, I didn't have to fight for my dreams, they stayed hidden in the essence of my being. (Confessed Tadeu Barbosa)

"What is gone is gone. I and my father offer our hand to lift you again and take you to a land of milk and honey. I promise you, there is no more suffering, guilt or fear of being happy. (Promised the son of God)

"Up to now, everything appears to be a great utopia. I am going to know you and wait for more concrete results. (Tadeu Barbosa)

"Of course, be at easy, my friend. (Aldivan)

"God gives exactly what we deserve. For the efforts I have made, I achieved success and during all my life has been like that. We just need to focus and we will achieve the desired results, for Father God blesses us. Messias Escapuleto)

"I have not achieved many things but I have learned from my father to be persistent. It is worth a lot. (Emanuel Melkin)

"Brothers, my life has been full of ups and downs. My parents brought me up at the farm and when there was a good year there was happiness, parties aplenty, fireworks and dancing. When there was a drought, we didn't even have food to eat, we would go and work like a pack donkey to earn a little money. Time passed, I got married and when Catimbau was declared a national park, things became better. Nowadays, I make a living from the tourism working as a guide. (Paulo Lacerda)

"Very good. We have then concluded that giving up is a mistake. In the case of failure, we must revise our strategies and try again. In God's time, things will certainly be achieved. (The seer)

"Correct, great master. (Messias Escapuleto)

The conversation went for some more time about varied subjects.

When they become exhausted, at end of the evening, they are going to try to sleep adopting the reversal scale. The next day, they were going to know the next trail from that enchanted place. Till the next chapter.

Chapter 5- *Trail of the tradition*

The night passed quickly, dawn arrives and soon is early morning. Thanks to Lord, nothing has happened, for has it was mentioned a person stood alert protecting the others. It was something extremely necessary for the place was infested with wild and venomous animals, due the preserved nature of caatinga's environment, something very rare in that region. In most of the county places, nature was devastated due the population explosion that impelled the depredation of the natural resources.

Our dear friends, one by one are getting up and organizing themselves. While Messias Escapuleto, Paulo Lacerda and Tadeu Barbosa are fetching firewood from the woods, the great son of God and his savior of old, Emanuel Melkin wait patiently cleaning up the ground around the tent. The two young men have a quick chat.

"How time flies, Aldivan. Since our meeting in Arcoverde, we are no longer the same. We have discovered in you the legendary master of the light, hope for mankind in these difficult times and who would have said that I, a mere sinner, would have saved from death when you were crossing the corner. How the world is full of surprises! (Emanuel Melkin)

"It was marked to happen in our destiny, my friend. I thank my father for us to have met each other and our new series. Together we can make history and transform people relationships between themselves and with it help the planet's evolution. I believe! (Aldivan)

"Yes, me too. What has our loved Son of God done during the time we have been apart?

"I have been taking care of my private life: My job at the public service, my family relationship, my writing work concerning the main series "The seer". In this path, I have met various people and whenever possible I showed my personality and that of my Father. I could understand that the most of them were needing affection, attention, friends and someone who would listen to them. Many times, they are people not understood by their own relatives and as they cannot open dialogue they prefer not to speak and pretend that everything is well, although that is not true. In me, they find a real friend. A brother that loves them independently of what they were, or what they have not done and who believes in them. For that, in my fifth romance I declared that "I am ". And you? What have done of importance?

"Not much. I have continued to live with my father in the village of Jeritacò living our simple life. We were waiting for the moment when God would reunite us again.

"Oh, good. We are here together with the others and I hope to live up to everyone's expectations.

"Me too. I want to be a great mate and friend of yours forever.

"Thank you. I make your words mine.

"Amen!

The other adventurers have just come back from the woods and the conversation is interrupted. With the fire wood they have brought, the fuel, the matches and the utensils taken out of the backpacks the fire is lit and then Aldivan and Emanuel begin to prepare breakfast (scrambled eggs) the coffee which was their mandatory for the day. In a matter of minutes everything is ready and they take care in quenching hunger and desperation. Besides the natural noise of the woods, silence reigns.

Among mischief, chatting, the singing of the birds and a splendid view of the park surrounded by mountains, typical vegetation of caatinga and the abundant fauna they savor the food. There, each one had a special reason to commemorate: The Seer, teaching, to know new people and be reunited with important friends, the guide Paulo Lacerda to meet diverse personalities in his professional pleasure, Tadeu Barbosa, the problematic, hoping for a better future, Messias to experience the role of apprentice, Emanuel to reunite with his protégé. In truth, everything was going well and was producing good expectations, thanks to the emblematic attitudes and advice from the true son of God, hidden from the great media.

Together, the series sons of light team, was a cohesive group and prepared for great journeys. Catimbau, the headquarters of the second saga, was not chosen by chance. It was a sacred place where some time ago the seer had the pleasure to visit and was marked in his mind, heart and memories. Bringing his friends to this place was like bringing them to his own home, welcome them from the bottom of his heart, just as his father does with everyone. In this, rested his greatness and his grace.

As soon as they finish breakfast, they quickly get together and the guide gives them the new instructions. Going ahead, Paulo leads the others through the narrow and dangerous trails of the escarpment surrounded by abysms on both sides. Almost four hours were spent on the way, until reaching the separation of the trails and following a new direction.

Taking the right, they access rock formations, forests and finally the mountain range. They pitch the tent right there, among the geographic faults, they lit a new fire, cook rice and beans for lunch and when everything is ready, they replenish their energies. Thirty minutes later, they have finished and they are free for the day's debate.

"My friends, I want to talk to you about an important and serious subject, the way you run your life. What important choices did you have to make up till now? (The seer)

"I have made several. Each pain life has imposed on me, I had gotten up and continue to live my life. In the meantime, I could not help to accumulate "Wound scars" from those events. My objective in being here is to heal them or at least understand them and suffer less. (Tadeu Barbosa)

"Tadeu, I understand perfectly. I have also made important choices and others I deferred them. Every day, life make us face questions that require immediate decision-making. The important is to reflect hard and make the right choice. It is not always possible and is there that the scars act, inflicting us pain. However, I guarantee you unlimited support in its causes and together we will analyse in this journey what is the best for you and the group in general. Is that right? (The son of God)

"Understood. We await the next happenings. (Tadeu)

"There are choices and sub-choices. The choices give you sufficient margin to deliberate and choose the most palpable way. It was so when I got married and became a guide. The sub-choices tie you up in such a way that leave you with no option. For example, when I was young, the fact that I was dependent on my father and he forbade me from studying, greatly setting back my life. Nowadays, I have got no strength to fight and change this reality. (Paulo Lacerda)

"I agree, Paulo. I only feel sad for your decision of giving up studying. There are insane mistakes and sane mistakes. The fact of not being able to study in the past does not impede your fight in the present. If you want, there is still time. (Aldivan)

"The situation has changed a lot, son of God. Nowadays, I am married man, I have a full-time job and I worry about the small children. I simply don't have the strength to change my past. (Paulo)

"We always find an excuse when we afraid of breaking taboos and confront our dilemmas. However, I respect your decision. (Seer)

"Thank you. That shows your spirit greatness. (Paulo Lacerda)

"All of us have got great choices to make, from small ones to big ones. What we do with our choices makes all the difference. (Messias Escapuleto)

"It is true. We have got no other option but to choose. With the acquired experience, the right choices are going to supersede the errors. (Aldivan)

"Exactly, master. Take care of the scars caused by the mistakes, that is the challenge. (Messias)

"I am here for that. (The son of God)

"Just as well. Glory to the father! (Messias)

"Master, I have also made many mistakes in my choices. What is the secret to reach the highest precision? (Emanuel Melkin Escapuleto)

"As I have already said, the experience. Another important reason is to analyses well the situation and make a list of priorities at that moment. They will show the way to follow. (Aldivan)

"Perfect. I will do that. Thank you. (Emanuel)

"Be focused and priorities, friends. Look at my example: I already have suffered poverty, rejection, unemployment, abandonment, indifference, loveliness, the lack of faith of those that surrounded me. However, all the time I believed in myself and in the father, who loves me so much. Each phase of your life has got something to be enjoyed, in my childhood I played, in the adolescence and youth I studied and, in my adulthood, I am focused on my work, on the social activities and on the relationships. Everything points to success, for I am determined, then learn from me and fight for your actual objective. (Taught the son of God).

"I will do that. (Tadeu)

"We too. Isn't it guys? (Messias)

"Yes. (The others)

"Very good. Let's rest now and plan the next steps. The adventure is not over yet. (The seer)

They obey command of the leader of the group and divide themselves for several activities. Aldivan, Messias and Paulo talk about the next steps of the journey. Emanuel and Tadeu go for a walk and fetch firewood. On their return, they get together again, prepare the fire and rest. Later, they cook, have diner and spend the rest of the evening in the tent because the temperature was very low.

At the end of evening, they will try to sleep amidst a flood of emotions. What else would it lie ahead? Continue to follow, readers.

Chapter 6- Trail through caatinga

Taking it in turns as always, our adventurers spend the night at that sanctuary. The moment required a profound reflection of everything that has been accomplished up to then: From the meeting at Arcoverde until the park at Buíque, they have already advanced a great deal in terms of evolution and the responsible for it, was named father God.

Independently of the gigantic challenge that was to live with their own pain, they were learning the rhythm of coexistence and the face of the place, the wild nature of caatinga which spread out in all the directions. It had been a great alternative, the walk in that park and the subsequent decision-making to which they had been subjected would not be such a catastrophe. On the contrary, it was something extremely necessary that the son of God would make a point of stressing.

The group has a clear impression that their wishes are taken shape and become reality in that beautiful wild awakening: On the North side, one can see the greatness of the mountain of Catimbau; on the South side, the smallness of the village of the same name; in the West, the jungle that spreads out for kilometers; in the East, the Canyon between mountains, a valley that in remote past housed a sea arm, where in the middle appears a resplendent sun. The view is simply spectacular and they ask themselves whether they are really on Earth or in a paradise in a supposed seventh dimension.

Everything is indeed fantastic: The surrounding people, the nature and the challenge itself. In good spirits, our adventurers rise early from the tent, lit again the fire with the remaining fire wood, prepare some boiled eggs and when ready they help themselves. While eating, they engage in small talk.

"We begin another day. Is it everything alright with you, guys? (The son of God)

"I feel like I have never felt before. It was about time that I had a trip like this, for it renews the strength and expands the options. I don't feel old. (Messias Escapuleto)

"Oh, so good. But don't feel old. Man is not measured by the grey hairs, but by his wisdom. (Aldivan)

"I know, I know. You say that because you are still in your thirties. Let you reach my age. (Retorted Messias Escapuleto)

"When I reach your age, is for I have learned much and lived long. I will never feel old. (Replied the son of God)

"Very good. (Sighed Messias)

"I also feel very good walking here. Walking beside such special people and with the nature it is a dream of four out five persons. I feel honored. (Emanuel Melkin Escapuleto)

"It is me who feel honored for having my savior by my side. If were not for you, I would have been smashed to pieces by that moving vehicle. You were a real guardian angel in my life. (Aldivan)

"Don't mention it! I am only a servant. Your real protector is Uriel, the Super-powerful prince of the main celestial militia. (Emanuel) "Don't tell me that. I am missing him and I am happy with your humility. If you need anything, my friend, I am at your disposal. (The seer made himself available)

"Thank you. I truly reciprocate. (Emanuel)

"I, know. (Added Aldivan)

"Coming here is being a great adventure. Having been destroyed several times by the facts of life, I didn't have anybody else to turn to. In an instant, I was hopeless and in another I am living special moments with true friends and with strangers who are now my friends. Little by little, I am losing the fear of being happy and at the end I hope to be free of my most secret anguishes. (Tadeu Barbosa)

"I am happy for that and very much wish that I will be able to transform your "still resistant Darkness" into pure light. My Father has done that with me and I firmly believe that I can do the same for you and for all humankind that believes in my name. It is only needed a little patience, tolerance and perseverance. We will get there, my friend. (Promised the seer)

"I hope so. Thanks for everything. (Tadeu Barbosa)

"Don't mention it. (The seer)

"Everything seems like a crazy dream to me. I have never had a group so unusual: A master, two friends, a problematic and me among all this oscillating with the facts. Caramba! I never thought that my job as a guide would bring such solid knowledge about human relationships. I want to learn more with you and to participate in some way in the success that will come, for I believe we are special. (Paulo Lacerda)

"Certainly, each one here has got a life story and can add something good for the mutual knowledge. Feel embraced by me and all, and I hope you will take us to places even more fantastic than this. (Aldivan)

"Yes, I will do it with the outmost pleasure. (Paulo Lacerda)

"Paulo, out of curiosity where are you going to take us today? (Asked the nervous Emanuel)

"Today we are going to walk a trail through caatinga, the most difficult of all. I recommend that you wear thick clothes and sun screen to face the thorns and the scorching sun. (Paulo Lacerda)

"Ok. (Emanuel)

"Guys, let's not waste time. Let's prepare as Paulo advised and as soon as we are ready, we will depart. There is a lot to do today. (The seer)

"Ok. (The others)

Everyone obeyed the leader's command. Looking for in their backpacks, they put on thick clothes and share some sun screen that they had brought. After, they pulled down the tent, keep it in one of the backpacks, walk a few hundred meters and move away from the natural faults. Turn right and enter a very narrow trail in the thick woods. The dangerous crossing of the caatinga's trail starts there.

At this moment, the feeling is of togetherness and peace despite the great difficulties. They have made up a great team, the sons of light, commanded by the father, represented by the seer. The son of God had the confidence and the necessary faith of his servants to act. By his command, they go ahead on the narrow trail for about a kilometer and take the first rest. With five minutes of rest, they take advantage to drink and receive instructions from the guide. After this lapse, they restart the walking.

Turning left in the thick woods, they follow another even narrower trail. As they advance, they are hit by tree branches and lacerating thorns. Then the guide provides a large knife and the situation improves a little. A kilometer in front, they pass through a fruit wood and some take advantage to feed themselves with the fruits and swinging on the trees. This activity takes them back to the childhood of several of them, causing a healthy longing. Soon after, they firmly continue the walk in the previous direction.

Advancing quickly, they complete the remaining distance to the center point of the trail of caatinga: A spacious clearing around the mountain and prodigious natural faults. Immediately, they pitch the tent, bring firewood from the woods and lit the fire to cook lunch. The day's menu is the traditional rice and beans accompanied the bird meat, from birds killed in the forest. It takes them about one and a half hour to have everything ready. In community, they dish out the food to one another in silence. In that immense green expansion, what was more important was the interaction between themselves, despite the constant danger and the uncertainties that they were being subjected to. However, the trip was well worth it.

The lunch finished, the seer got amidst them and started talking, initiating the day's debate.

"Brothers, I want to touch on a crucial point for many people, their attitude face to the difficulties. I am using myself as a parameter. I was born and grew up in a retrograde ambient, in the rural Northeast still archaic, that is, society expect from you but not always is possible to come up to this expectation. During a great part of my life, I close myself in my own world, denied my own will and this was a great mistake, for it only brought me sadness and unhappiness. I wanted to turn myself into a person that would please my family but didn't work out. When I freed myself, I was rejected, despised and humiliated by people, but I felt good. Now I am the same and I taught in my best-seller "I am", the fifth saga of the series "the seer", how to arouse this side. I am still not happy with my choices but I am sure I am on the way. Could you also share some of your personal experience?

"I know very well what that is. Indeed, most of us live subdued by a so-called moral society. Some of us confront it and other simply accept its rules and this lot is the majority. The fear is great. In my case, I have always been a model of dedication and never strayed from the common norm, thus I didn't have any problem in being accept, despite the traps in life. (Stated Tadeu Barbosa)

"What you have just described is simply inspiring. I am proud of having been your master and now your servant. Congratulations for your courage. In my personal life, I have already come across several of those situations. In some, I took a risk and in others I guarded myself. There were right decisions and mistakes that taught me to be the man that I am today. With my experience, I can say: The freedom that we have got is the best thing given to us by the creator. We are made by those choices. (Messias Escapuleto)

"My father always taught me to make my own decisions regardless of suffering or not, I am the author of my own history. (Emanuel Melkin Escapuleto)

"I am happy, my friends. It took me a while longer to understand it, but finally I took a decision. Nowadays, I can walk with my head high. Paulo, and your experience, how was it? (Aldivan)

"It was similar to your situation, a very strict and retrograde family, but luckily, I didn't have anything to hide. The only bad thing is that I didn't have the opportunities the youth of today has got. I was born an ass and grew up as an ass. (Paulo)

"I understand, but I have already said that there is something that can be changed. All you need is to be willing. (The seer)

" I, know. But for the reasons already mentioned, it is not possible. Paulo)

"Ok. (The seer)

"What else does your book say? (Emanuel)

"Thirteen stories, a dreamer, a youth and two archangels searching for the truth. What have a depressed person, a pedophile, an abortionist, a drug addict, a professional player, scientists, criminals, a sexologist, a schizophrenic and a handicapped have in common? All of them trying to reflect on their actions, their future paths beside the seer, a special and revolutionary being, on a great journey in the Brazilian Northeast. Presenting himself as the son of God, he promises to listen to all of them, advise them and give them valuable tips as how to restart their lives revealing along the time his personality and that of his Father. The main objective is to awaken the internal "I am" in each one of them and by reaching this miracle, the truth will be finally revealed. "I am" also represents a cry of freedom in face of the social restraints, an example of what Jesus has done in the past. "I am" shows in this way how the true human being is in contradiction with those that are used to judge the others. (The Seer)

"Wonderful, I am a fan of yours and I want this book. I am also proud of being part of an important series, "Sons of light". (Emanuel)

"Thank you for your support. It is for you who is a part of the universe of my readers, for my father and for all humankind that I continue to persist with my dream. Everything will be alright, I have faith! (The son of God)

"Amen. (Everybody in a gesture of support)

"Well, let's take care of other tasks. (Aldivan)

The talk ends and each one went to take care of their responsibilities towards the group. During the rest of the afternoon and the evening, they occupy themselves in different ways. At the end of the day, they rest already thinking of the next trail.

Chapter 7- Trail of Caiana

Another day begins in the beautiful park of Catimbau. Very early, our dear adventurers get up and come out of the improvised tent. Well organized, they prepare the morning meal and when it's ready they share it equally. The moment requires silence and great concentration from everybody's side due to the great challenge of walking the next trail and evolve in relation to the healing of the wound scars.

During breakfast, they look with complicity as if they knew each other for centuries. The team of the series sons of light was stronger than ever. Emanuel takes the chance to break the silence.

"Paulo, what is the next step?

"Today, we are going to walk the trail Caiana, a trail restricted to researchers and adventurers. It is a short trail, but complicated. (Paulo Lacerda)

"Right. We are ready, aren't we guys? (Emanuel)

"Yes, of course. I fully trust our team. (The seer)

"If we are in the rain, is to get wet. (Tadeu Barbosa)

"There is nothing that our will cannot overcome. (Messias Escapuleto)

"Very well. I like to see, willingness. Don't worry about anything, I will guide you in all directions. (Paulo)

"Thank you. (Aldivan)

The small talk ended right there and our friends took care in finishing the meal, good scrambled eggs and tropical fruit. A while later, having finished the meal and following instructions from the operations commanders, they gather their things and dismantle the tent. With everything ready, they exit the clear where they were and head to the point where the trails' part.

On the way, walking along the narrow trail they have several surprises: They almost step on snake which was chased away by the guide, meet another group of adventurers and greet them, some have stomach problems due to the food in the forest and the walk must be suspended for a while. Restarting the walk, they go straight ahead until they arrive at the fork in the road. Two hours have passed since they have started walking and they are happy to conquer another stage. Now, all it is needed is to remain on the trail.

On the new trail, already inside Caiana, they felt comfortable and happy despite the natural difficulties imposed by the woods. Everything is worth the pain for the sake of knowledge and the mutual amusement. After eight hundred meters, they come across to the first landscape of note: Three natural faults, worked by nature on the rocks along millennium, surrounded of vegetation and the imposing mountain in the Northeast direction. Standing out in the wild forest, the geologic formations take the shape of a ship, of a toast and another of a tower.

The visitors are speechless for a few moments face this marvel of nature. They feel small in front of the mystery, the life and the nature created by Aldivan's Father. Talking about the son of God, the reason to bring them here was exactly that: To show the simplicity and greatness of nature and parallel to this heal everybody's wounds with insight and intelligence. The strategy seemed to be working.

A little later, they are obliged to restart the walk because of the time. Led by the guide, they advance a bit more and the obstacles are gradually overcome. The next liberating landscape appears: A set of stones, bowl and lid, decorated with rock paintings. Looking at the paintings they find one depicting a tiger, another of a bird eating fruit and the third one representing the figure of a man. They feel graced by a miracle, vestiges of ancestors from millions of years ago, completely preserved on the stone. Delicately touching the paintings, they imagine their lives, their culture and the earth of that era. It is simply fantastic.

A short while later, they start walking again in search of new adventures. The trail gets even narrower giving a suffocating sensation. Being there was really a miracle due to the great difficulties faced. After six hundred meters, they reach another natural work of art: A triangular mountain, with numerous massifications and ramifications, probably caused by the exposure to the rain and sun. It is located at the center of the plain. Our friends take the chance to take some photos, rest a little and receive information from the guide. After this quick interval, the walk continues.

The part of the walk becomes more complicated due to everybody being tired. They decrease the rhythm and, in that way, they enjoy better the region's view, that without a doubt was one of most beautiful in the world. At end of the journey, they arrive at the edge of the abysm, the biggest rock formation, from where they can see the canyon spreading out in all directions. Wow! Simply spectacular. By mutual consent, they pitch the tent there and start work in their activities. Initially, all of them engage in the preparation of the lunch that offers as menu couscous and wild chicken. Well organized, our friends finish the meal in about one and half hours. They help one another and as usual the discussion starts at that moment.

"I take the opportunity to commence a discussion about the work in general. For about six years my career has been public servant and two years in my actual post. My impression about my work is the best possible: I have got a monthly salary, stability, cool work colleagues, an understandable chief, possibilities of salary increase, I like the work I do and better still, this job allows my second job as a writer, for it is only six hours of work per day. In other words, I am happy. And your situation? How is it? (The son of God)

"I am satisfied with work as a guide. But I have had many problems in my life: I have faced poverty, the droughts, I have also suffered harassment by the boss. So, everything I have suffered has left memorable marks in my body and in my mind leaving me more skeptical about the work. (Paulo Lacerda)

"I know how you feel, Paulo. I also have suffered a little of that. It is not by chance that I am son of simple farmers. The hardships that I faced made me stronger and more focused on my objectives. Today, I am in a good job because I deserve it. (Aldivan)

"Congratulations. "I am" who "I am" and I love you unconditionally, with this love extended to all humanity. Don't worry, brother. (The seer)

"Amen. Thank you very much. (Paulo)

"I am self-employed and my life is not easy on account the drought that plagues this region since 2012. Our salvation are the casual jobs that we do which hardly let us survive. (Related Messias Escapuleto)

"My situation is the same as my fathers'. (Emanuel Melkin Escapuleto)

"What can say to you? Nothing that is happening is my fault or my fathers'. Largely, they are natural reactions of the environment to the modern man's contact who only thinks of producing and destroying. We are suffering the consequences for an indeterminate time. I am not rich, but in case you need help I will make an effort. Count on me, my friends. (The seer made himself available)

"I thank you for understanding, son of Yahweh. Don't worry about us, there will always be a way out. (Messias)

"I am happy for you feeling good about your work and I hope you will continue to transform the lives of many people. (Emanuel)

"Thank you both. You are rare examples of devoted servants.

Emanuel, I don't forget our first meeting. It was something really striking. (Aldivan)

"Me neither. Saving you from the danger made me reborn as a man. Today, I really feel very happy. (Emanuel)

"I am also very happy for everything my father has provided me with up to now. I am a young man accomplished at work, writer and with many friends and loyal servants. For you and all the readers I will continue with my work. (Aldivan)

"So, I wish. (Emanuel)

"Amen (The seer)

"My life is stagnant. At this moment, I am beginning to feel hopeful and the perspectives are pointing to self-growing. However, I will have to wait longer to resolve serious internal problems. (Commented Tadeu Barbosa) "We are here to help you, my friend. In passing, we learn more face this nature spectacle that is Catimbau. Everything is possible. All is needed is to be patient and have faith. (The son of God)

"I believe. For that reason, I am staying with you. (Tadeu Barbosa)

"Then this is it, my friends: Work is an important part of our life reflecting itself in the other spheres, for example, in the personal and social ones. Anything else to add on? (The seer)

"Only to mention that we are on the right way. I have already learned a lot. (Messias)

"For that, our team must be congratulated. Our work in the literature reflects in our personal aspect. (Emanuel)

"Gosh! My wife must be already missing me. Tools of the trade. (Paulo Lacerda)

"As I have got nobody, everything is alright. I want to restart my social life after this adventure. (Tadeu)

"Excellent. We are together. Let's continue the day's activities. (Concluded the seer)

Obeying the expedition leader, they finish the lunch and after, they divide themselves into tasks. Paulo and Aldivan plan the next steps of the adventure and exchange important information while the others rest. Late afternoon, they wake up, prepare dinner, and when it is ready, they have the last meal of the day. Later, they all go to bathe in a nearby lagoon. On their return, they lit the fire, admire the stars and tell interesting jokes. Late into the evening, employing the rotation schedule they go to sleep. The next day would bring more discoveries to our group. Continue accompanying us.

Chapter 8- Trail of the little mountain

Dawn and the start of a new day present great challenges. First, during the night a scorpion bit Emanuel causing great pain, which only passed by taking some medicine. Close to dawn, a python came near the camp and only didn't injury somebody because Messias was on guard duty and redirect it back to nature. Phew! Our friends were safe.

Waking up in good spirits, our friends prepare the appetizing chicken eggs accompanied by tropical fruit representing a real banquet. Everything is ready in a jiff and is served in equal portions. The food is quickly devoured for the exhaustion was obviously at an extreme level, as they have had several days of long walks away from home.

In the meantime, the unique coexistence with the son of God and with those wise beings of light was changing in a definitive way the lives of Tadeu Barbosa and Paulo Lacerda. At each step taken by them, the wisdom of the three emanated as if was coming from the creator and was contagious to the others. Everything was worthwhile.

While they eat, they attentively listen to Paulo's observations about the next trails. Paulo takes the opportunity to highlight the difficulties which are increasing due to everyone's physical exhaustion, and also praises their mood despite not being used to this type of programmed. The others thank him for his words.

With everything defined, without major problems they finish breakfast. Once the meal is finished, at the asking of the seer, the new walk begins. Looking towards the abysm of the canyon in a gesture of goodbye, and after exchanging position the son of God and Paulo command the operation. The search for a short cut in the dense woods, as a way of quickly reach the separation of the two trails.

With Paulo's experience, they not only reach the short cut, but make the trip in an efficient way. The result is that they are already at the new trail, the little mountain, with only a few scratches.

Advancing in a single file, they access the first touristic spot of this area: A clearing full of flowers and creepers. The effect is so strong that it looks like a western film at the cinema. The place, apart from being spectacular, spreads all around. They take the opportunity to rest a little, take some photos and thank God for the marvelous view. According to the guide, the best is still to come.

A few minutes later, they continue their walk in a rapid and organized way. After over an hour of effort they pass through rock formations, bromeliads, "umbu", cacti, "angico", "catingueira" and other vegetal specimens surrounding the trail. They access a place of transition and soon after they come across the greatest marvel seen up to now: A lake of fresh water surrounded by rocks with a waterfall.

They seize the opportunity to drink water, that must be said was very clean. After, they bathe and play in the water. Being there was more than a gift, it was a present from the creator for those creatures who had already suffered so much in life.

The relaxation time lasts half an hour and they come out of the water, they stand around it. By general consent, they decide to camp there for the rest of the day. As it was near lunch time, they prepare the day's menu which consists of tropical soup. With simple ingredients, the dish is ready without much refinement. Just as well that there was nobody with freshness and was not going to complain.

Apart from the meal they reserve the lunch time for an internal reflection. Thirty minutes later, a new meeting was marked for a debate with the view of the members to get to know each better. The talk is then initiated:

"I propose a reflection about ourselves and the way we manage our friendships. What have got to share? (Enquired the seer)

"My family is Italian and are used to value the family and friends. Since I have known people, I have always put it into practice and taught it to my son. (Revealed Messias Escapuleto)

"Exactly. I have learnt those values from my father and I always try to put them into practice. The proof of that is the fact that I saved you from a great tragedy. (Emanuel Melkin Escapuleto)

"Oh, my wonderful and great friends. I admire you. Together, we make up the sons of light trinity. I thank in special Emanuel for having saved me from death and his father for having taught for some time. I also act in that way, I always try to know new people, make friends and interact with respect for everyone. Thank God, the few friends I have got are loyal and among them I include you. (The son of God)

"Thank you, my good boy. (Said Messias)

"Marvelous. (Emanuel Escapuleto)

"I have never been inclined to make sincere friendships. I was brought up in the strictness of a family that advocated the isolation from others. The most I had were either companions or colleagues. However, with you, I have discovered the real value of friendship and if you allow me, I already consider you as my friends. (Paulo Lacerda)

"All of those that I considered as friends abandon me. How to say? I feel that friendship ought to be and a two-ways street with respect and understanding from both sides. (Tadeu Barbosa)

"I understand how you feel. Paulo, I am happy for having awaken in you this noble feeling of friendship, I am honored. Tadeu, the best for you is to forget the past once for all, to give your cause to me and my father and then the miracle will happen. (The son of God)

"The time has not arrived yet. Let's be patient. (Tadeu)

"Yes, I will wait for the right time. (Aldivan)

"Thank you. (Tadeu)

"My friends, changing the subject, what do you think of the modern relationships? (The seer)

"Very different from the past, nowadays having sex between couples still in courtship is more liberal. (Messias)

"Ever more people are focused on the materialism than on the relationship itself. (Stated Emanuel)

"Very good observation from Messias. But in some regions some customs still prevail such as the virginity of the women. (Paulo)

"I, know. In general, in the villages of the interior. I agree. (Messias)

"This subject revives my wound scars and for that reason I prefer not to comment. (Lamented Tadeu)

"Sure. You are all right. I will add that ever growing sexual trivialization is going to put a distance between the human being and God. Furthermore, the marriages are evermore scarce. Those that will survive, a great part will be destroyed by the natural civilization's phenomena. The future promises to be complicated. (Concluded the son of God)

"And how are you doing? Talking of feelings? (Enquired Messias)

"Well, I am not used to talk about my personal life with anybody, but you are my friends. I am looking for something else in a relationship, that feeling of the old days that is evermore forgotten. I want the original Aleph, and consequently I do not get satisfied with very little or with relationships purely carnal. (The seer)

"In conclusion: You are single. (Emanuel)

"Bull's eye. (The seer)

"No problem. Whatever your father has written it will happen. Have faith. (Messias)

"True, my friend. This is not my main concern. Right now, I am happy, for God has blessed me with a great mission. So, everything is very good. (The seer)

"OK. Just as well. (Messias)

"Great son of God! I am thinking of the recent events that involved our group and that has aroused my curiosity. At no time, I have heard you complaining about us or your father. What is the secret? (Paulo Lacerda)

"The personal philosophy of feeling how much I can expect from others. It all comes down to observation and control. At right moment, I will act. (Aldivan)

"Brilliant. (Paulo)

"I cannot wait for the time when my heart will meet with yours and with the world. (Tadeu)

"I thank you for the opportunity. There is a right time for everything. (The seer)

"Amen. (Tadeu)

"Well, my friends, let's stop for now. Go and take care of the details, for I want a celebration tonight. Today, is a very special day. OK? (The seer)

"Yes. (The others in agreement)

The seer's command is accepted. They quickly get together and hand out the tasks. The afternoon was long and would serve to get ready for the preparation of the expected evening. In preparation, they search for firewood in the woods, find it, return to camp, make and lit the fire and cook typical dishes. They wait for a while. With everything ready, at eighteen hours, the celebration commences with food and drinks. While they eat the talk flows freely among them.

"What is the reason for the celebration, great seer? (Tadeu Barbosa)

"We are celebrating the gift of life and the fact of being with you. It is rare occasion and we must take advantage of it. (The seer)

"Sure. You should know that nothing makes sense to me and consequently I don't have much to celebrate. (Tadeu)

"I understand perfectly. But I stress that we are here as a group. The main objective is for us to understand and heal one another. (The seer)

"I, know. I am waiting for the next events. (Tadeu)

"Sure. (The son of God)

"Son of God, what is the great secret relating to the wound scars? (Messias)

"There is no secret. I think that the main issue is called experience and control. I am a human being who have already suffered much and I live daily with many difficulties. They made me learn to be stronger and more decisive. My life reached a point where I have decided not to suffer anymore and carried this flag to the last consequences. It came right. (The son of God)

"Brilliant. You are indeed a unique being. How good to have you beside us. (Messias)

"Thank my father, for he is the one who determine my steps. Exactly as in that day that I was saved from a tragedy, do you remember, Emanuel? (The son of God)

"I remember as if it were today. That lorry almost destroyed our lives. Just as well that I was quick. (Emanuel)

"I will never forget that favor, nor the benefactor. A special place in my kingdom it is reserved for you. (The son of God)

"Amen. Thank you! (Emanuel)

"I also want one. (Messias)

"Is there a place for me? (Paulo Lacerda)

"I intend to enter it. (Tadeu Barbosa)

"Brothers, I think it is great the interest showed by you. I wish that all the human beings were like that. In my kingdom, there is place for the entire world. It is enough to follow the old commandments and the new alliance and put your despair in the hands of my Father. It was Him who create us and completely transform the world. Nothing is impossible for those who believe in the name of God alive and in the names of his sons. (Aldivan)

"Amen! Glory! (Everybody)

"Let's continue the celebrations and happiness for everybody. (The seer)

With this statement, the son of God concluded the conversation and obeying the master the party carried on for a while longer. They danced, made mischief, satisfied their physiologic needs and admired the starry sky of that paradise. Catimbau was a striking place, full of beauty and mysteries. Those that visit it will never forget it. All the surrounding environment was helping with treatment and the unfolding of the events which principal objective was to recuperate them from their pain. Would it be possible, the complete healing of the wound scars, as the son of the Father had promised or was, he only gaining time and duping them all? The others were about to discover, for the adventure on the trail was coming to an end.

At the end of the evening, they go to sleep. We await the next day. Let's go forward with the narrative.

Chapter Nine – Trail of the Canyon

A new day dawns for our dear friends. They wake up almost simultaneously and between them they organize the different tasks. That day was a special colorful and dazzling for them. They have been in the dense woods for some days and little by little they were reaping the fruits of their work: The interaction and friendship between them was tight, they have recovered the lost hope and faith, and the future was promising. All this thanks to a spectacular being deservingly called son of God. Despite the title of authority, he was simple, humble and above all human.

The seer stands up for a moment after he had made his contribution to the breakfast preparation: Tapioca, biscuits and coffee. Smoothing his hair, ruffling his silk shirt and checking the consistence of his high black boots he observes his servants for a while. For them, he had once more left behind the home comfort, the work and his colleagues and his neighbors. He had only not abandoned the readers who accompany him in this adventure, which was the second saga of the series" Sons of light".

With his gift and with his followers he was exerting himself to find a way out, in face of another great challenge: Healing the "Wound scars" of someone who has only failed along his life. By analogy, he would heal the others' problems and all humankind, for he had feedback for it.

Eating! Tadeu calls him to have breakfast with his friends, and he responds immediately. They make a circle and help themselves to the available food. In an atmosphere of peace and harmony, to eat was a sacred ritual that nothing could interrupt. And so, thirty minutes pass by.

Later, they got up, dismantle the tent, pack the backpacks and depart immediately in search of a new adventure, the last one in the region of the village of Catimbau. Following a known trail, they leave the lake behind, where they had experienced an incredible feeling. Certainly, they would carry this moment through their entire life.

The next objective was the trail of the Canyon, one of the most famous and beautiful trails of the park. To get there they would have to pass the transition line which separated the two trails and which was quite lengthy. They needed an hour of continuous walk to pass the divide.

Having made the crossing, they look for the trail's first calling card. Led by the guide, they go forwards through the caatinga's exuberant vegetation which flanked both sides. The first stop is to get to know a rare and endemic specimen: Atilansia Catimbauense, a species of bromeliad, unique on the planet. The beauty and simplicity of the plant impress them all and some take the opportunity to take photos.

Later, they continue the walk. Now, the trail presents some detours which must be closely followed to avoid getting lost. The Park was enormous and treacherous to the inexperienced. Three hundred meters ahead, they have the first view of the natural geologic faults. A pair of elevations, a pointing one and another broader, the latter resembling an elephant and the first one an eagle ready to fly. The view was simply wonderful.

The biggest problem was that time was limited and they could not stop. There was still a lot of ground to cover. Aware of this, they carry on steadily on their walk. The next important stop comprising of two monuments: A set of rock formations divided into a rectangular area and a unique formation in the shape of a tortoise shell. The guide explains their probable origin and the way how to preserve them. Each one pays attention to the information and details of the monuments and take care to leave intact.

A little later, they continue from where they have stopped. A few hundred meters after one of the greatest beauties of the planet was awaiting them: Made of great sandstone walls, the Canyon is held as one of the best visual representations of the park of Catimbau. They reach the edge of the abysm and some risk to sit at the edge contemplating the divine work. How great and wonderful was God, for having created such beautiful things.

Many are lost for words at that place, which was making the "wound scars" disappear instantly. The miracle was made due to what many call the sacred ground. In a quick reunion, our friends decide to camp nearby and in their last night under the sky of Catimbau in the region of Buíque.

Later, they gather firewood, lit the fire and begin to prepare lunch for the insatiable travelers. At that time, they are thirsty and hungry due the effort made during the walk.

Cooking a meal based on chicken, our adventurers show their culinary expertise and when ready they savor it. The food is well season and tastes good.

They begin to feed themselves enjoying the food. The sun appears in the middle of the sky of Catimbau, shining its powerful rays on our unprotected adventure companions. The five of them and the thriving nature make a perfect picture worthy of Da Vinci.

The lunch unfolds among mischief, faces, smiles, in a perfect interaction between themselves, what was normal after days together. They made a perfect and competent team worthy of success.

The lunch finished; they were ready for another interesting debate.

"I still don't understand the fact that I am not happy. What I have done to deserve this, Son of God? (Tadeu Barbosa)

"You have done nothing, brother. Forget the past. From now on, it is another story which is going to be made and in it, victory is guaranteed. (The seer)

"Taken. Amen! (Tadeu Barbosa)

"And you, are you happy, son of God? (Paulo Lacerda)

"Yes, I am happy in my mission together with the father. All the rest will be added on, for I am good, obedient and loyal. It is a question of time, I believe! And you? (The son of God)

"I wish I had your faith! (Tadeu)

"After a long and difficult journey, I live with my family and there nothing better. (Paulo)

"I and my father we fight together for survival. Thus, everything is well. (Emanuel)

"God is a star in our life and as my son said we are two warriors. (Messias)

"As the nostalgic Rui Barbosa said, "worse than the sadness of not having conquered it is the shame of not having fought" and you will not go through this. Never give up on your dreams, friends. (Aldivan)

"Amen! (The others)

"What to say about you? You are the spring that propels my life, my projects and my adventures. Nothing makes sense without your support and that of the readers. I thank you for the trust and the dedication in every page of this book. (Aldivan)

"I also take the opportunity to thank everyone, your company is superb beside this wild nature. (Tadeu Barbosa)

"Everything started with your phone call asking for help. I and my son decided to help you and our path ended up crossing the path of the son of God. It was perfect. (Messias) "As if crossing that corner, the son of God would not be there?! (Emanuel)

"True. Everything is written. (Agreed the seer)

"And I have complemented the team with my experience of the woods. We are five champions. (Paulo Lacerda)

"The mere fact that we are here already shows our resolve. The success will come by consequence. Glory to my father! (Aldivan)

"Glory! (The others)

"Son of God, I have got only one day to accompany you in this great adventure. I need to return to my family. Are you interested in getting to know the trail of the great fortress, in Ibimirim? (Paulo)

"I am very interested. This will close our adventure with a key of gold. Do you agree, guys? (The seer)

"Agreed. (Emanuel)

"Amen. (Tadeu)

"Your decision is a command. (Messias)

"Then it is decided. We will depart then. (The seer)

Immediately after this talk, they dismantled the tent and went packing the backpacks. When everything is ready, they take a short cut in the woods. The aim was to reach the vehicle near the initial trail. Despite the considerable distance, with Paulo's knowledge they make the journey in record time. Exactly at thirteen hours they return to the vehicle and start descending the mountain towards the village.

On the descent, they come to the road and consequently with civilization. How we missed the modern life! Impelled by the desire to know even more they arrive at Catimbau, they make a quick stop for lunch and after they go straight on the road towards the municipality of Ibimirim. It is there that the final sprint of the story was going to unfold.

Chapter ten – The trail of the great Wall

Ibimirim is about 110(one hundred and ten) kilometers from the municipality of Buíque. On the way there, our friends take the chance to rest and enjoy themselves the best way possible. It was a moment of great peace and harmony after so many days in the dense woods. The five participants in the adventure felt refreshed and optimistic about the last stage of this journey with much more to come.

In special, the seer and Tadeu, who have a good rapport between themselves. It was only a matter of time and the right moment for things to be finally put right. In relation to the others, they have also learned a lot with everything that has happen. As a result, they will never be the same again.

Catimbau thus showed to be a sacred place, for it had produced a true miracle in everyone's life. The future promised even more for everyone. All it was needed was to have a little faith in God and in themselves.

The total time spent on the trip was one hour and twenty minutes. They follow a dirt road that leads them to the nearest possible to the trail of the great wall. They Park the car, alight from it and begin the walk.

Following a narrow trail, our friends embark in the woods and feel the sensation of being in paradise. The great wall presents itself as a tall bush, macambiras, mulungus, umbuzeiros among other specimens. From the beginning of the trail until the first postcard is about one hundred meters. It consists of an intricated rock elevation made by nature, probably due the effect of the rain and sun. The rock mass extended for some meters giving a spectacular atmosphere to the environment. The tourists take the opportunity to take some photos beside the important monument. They take a breather and continue with walk.

A short distance ahead is the turn of admiring the harmonious enchanting peak. Located on the edge of a precipice and sided by the trail and vegetation, it stands out imposing and majestic. It is also worthy of stopping and take photos. Soon after, they restart the walk.

After another twenty minutes of vigorous walk, they stop for the day, for it was already getting late. The chosen place is beside an escarpment of hundreds of meters high. They proceed to pitch the tent, look for firewood, lit the fire, prepare dinner and eat as it is getting dark. The food stimulates them and renews their strength. Soon after, the seer stands in front of them all and starts the talking:

"Very well, my friends. We are at the last part of our little mischief. In this opportunity, you have had the chance to attain knowledge and this led you to important reflections. You also had the chance of knowing me better and reach your own conclusions. What do you have to say?

"I thank you for the time together. I and my son are evermore enchanted with you. Together, we make a beautiful series. (Messias Escapuleto)

"I hope so. (The seer)

"Thanks to god, we are in the right way and this mainly due to your presence. You have exceeded our expectations, son of God. (Emanuel Melkin Escapuleto)

"You have all been excellent too. We will be remembered for ever by our readers and we will give Catimbau it's due value. (The seer)

"Amen! (Emanuel)

"It is indeed impressive. In all my time as a guide, I have never seen a group like this. You have all my support to continue this endeavor. (Paulo Lacerda)

"You are absolutely right, my friend. These companions of ours are stars and they deserve to shine. There is only one thing missing: The acceptance of my person from our companion Tadeu. (The seer)

"It was missing! Now I am completely convinced that you are the best for me, my lord and master. What must I do now? (Tadeu Barbosa)

"Come to me! (The seer)

Tadeu does not hesitate in obeying. With sure steps, approaches the seer. With a broad smile, the master stretches his arms and touches the calloused hands of the servant. In an instant, nothing could separate them. With that friendly touch, the son of God was finally able to access the entire life of that noble colleague in a brief vision. Here it is:

The vision

Pesqueira, September 1974

Carmen Lucia Barbosa and Renato Tavares Barbosa, were coming back, on the first Sunday, from the hospital where they have been for almost twelve hours. The reason was the birth of couple's first and only son due to complications with the birth. They chose his name Tadeu deriving from the Latin Thaddaeus heart, chest, bosom and intimacy.

From the meadow until the neighborhood where they lived it took them ten minutes by their own car and were carrying with them the greatest prize, which was the son, a symbol of the couple's love. Everything would be different and with greater promises, for there, it was locked his blood and his power. But what destiny did that baby of light brown eyes carry? Only the future would tell, but for the time being they were not worried about it.

As soon as they arrived home, they pamper their son, and this would continue for some time. The mother was a housewife and the father got a week of leave from work. Everything was happiness in that family.

Childhood and pre-adolescence

The first week passed by, he first month, the first year and so on. Every step of little boy Victor was closely followed by his parents. From the baptism, the entrance to college, the school time, the walks and the trips in and outside town, the parents' meetings and the social events.

From a young age, he was brought up in accordance with the beliefs of the catholic faith and the values that a good man must have. Despite being quite clever, he seemed to assimilate well the teachings and had a tranquil life. A childhood that we could say of mischief, friends and colleagues and a pre-adolescence with necessary freedom to feel like a human being. Everything was pointing towards a normal life full of happiness.

The rebellion

The prison's village is a set of buildings very close to a prison at the town of Pesqueira, in such way that climbing over the its wall there was access to several houses.

It is an evening like any other. Tadeu and his parents took the opportunity to pay a visit to his grandparents who lived in the neighborhood. Exactly at eighteen hours they arrived at their residence, were welcomed and went in. They spend the evening talking, enjoying a rare moment due to commitments of both. It felt very good when such opportunity arose for, they were could enjoy the company of their only relatives living near the town.

Later, at twenty-two hours, the moment of saying goodbye and depart arrived. They said goodbye quickly, came out of the house and at this point something unusual happened: A rebellion erupted and several prisoners managed to escape from the prison. The confusion was all round, for the delinquents were prepared to do anything.

Tadeu and his parents tried to seek refuge at some house but realized that there was no time to do it. In a last resort, Tadeu's parents proceeded to a corner, and found enough old rags to protect their son. The wrapped him up a gave him instructions and departed at random.

Then Tadeu tried to stay quiet, as his parents have advised him. Sometimes, he heard murmurs nearby but he kept still. The night went by and dawn broke and finally was daytime. Gathering courage, the little boy got up anxious to know what had happened.

He saw then a desolating scenery: Blood, vestiges of bullets, houses invaded and smashed, policemen everywhere, a scenery of war. Getting in contact with the policemen, he identified himself and enquiring about his parents and grandparents, he was given a list of the people killed. Unfortunately, for his despair, his parents and grandparents had been assassinated. This first great shock was very profound in his little heart.

As he was a minor, the little boy was taken to a shelter where he would wait for adoption since he didn't have relatives who would take the responsibility to bring him up.

Despite of the kindness and good receptiveness of the place administrators, the little boy could not help thinking of the sad end of his relatives representing the first great "Wound scar" of his existence. Meantime, life continued. Good luck, little Tadeu.

Life at the shelter and the first dating

Tadeu remained in the shelter from twelve until eighteen years. In this intense and painful period and although pleasurable at certain times he lived through numerous situations: He finished the primary and medium school, made many friends, went on trips, participated in his first election. However, the most important event, was to have dated a girl, with whom he lived for about a year. She was also at the orphanage and when she reached majority found a job in another town, separating them forever.

Soon after, was Tadeu's turn of leaving and thanks to the help of a social programmed he found a job and returned to his parents' home. It was the best solution for the time being. In this way, his life continued.

The first official dating and the marriage

At his job which was at a grocer's shop Tadeu had the opportunity of getting to know many people among them work colleagues and clients. It was exactly there that he fell in love with Karen Lopes who worked as a cashier. As he worked as a packer, and there was always frequent contact between them and he fell for her tender and loving manner. The result: Dating for one year and subsequent marriage.

Once married they went to live at the same place, his parents old house. From then on, they began to build a life together. In the first years of marriage, they focused on their work and on the holidays, they took trips to nice places, that they could afford.

At the end of the fifth anniversary of their union, there was good news: Karen was expecting. Tadeu was very happy and made the most effort for his companion to have a safe pregnancy. There were nine months of preparation and anxiety until the son was born. After that one, in the following years two more sons arrived. Karen went for an operation becoming permanently sterile.

Together the five of them were happy for quite a while in a family atmosphere full of peace, prosperity and happiness. Will it last forever?

The tragedy

The life of Tadeu's family would change forever due to a tragic event. The case happened in the center of the town. Crossing the street, Karen was distracted and didn't notice a bus approaching at high speed. The collision was unavoidable and with an impact of this nature there was no chance of surviving.

She was recovered, identified and the husband informed. Lost for words, he made the arrangements for the funeral procedures, which took place in the same day. Accompanied by several acquaintances, the procession buried Karen's body amidst general shock. The word that best described the state of the spouse's mood, was despair.

Unsettled by the event, Tadeu abandon his job and the care of his own sons still in need protection and affection. He began to use drugs, was exposed and lost forever guardianship of beloved sons. After, frustrated, moved to Buíque where he promised himself to rebuild his life. However, the ghosts of the past were still tormenting him.

He remembered then a couple of friends that he had made in one of his travels and as he had their contact, he asked them for help. Emanuel and Messias departed then from Jeritacó, met the seer and the three made themselves available to help that poor soul. The result was a trip to Catimbau, the wild paradise that had made a miracle. Finally, Tadeu and his "Wound scars" settled their account and he was ready to continue his life forwards with his head held up high.

Return to reality

The vision disappears and the seer seems to be meditating a little about that situation. He needed to choose the right words and when he is sure of that, he makes contact:

"Very well, my loyal servant. I understood everything. What we must understand is all that belongs to a past that must be forgotten or at the least tolerated. The most important thing is the present moment and I can see that you have recovered most of your desire.

"Thanks to God and you, my friends. If weren't for your action in the moment of anxiety that I was going through I think I would not be here. It was what I needed: Sincere friends who would support me. I believe that my life is going to be better from now on and if by chance I suffer again I will know how to deal with it. (Tadeu Barbosa)

"Congratulations, Tadeu, I am happy for you. (Emanuel Melkin Escapuleto)

"Me too. Mission accomplished. (Messias Escapuleto)

"Tadeu rose an important question: The "Wound scars". I also have my own ones and I will take the opportunity to learn and control them. This journey was very profitable. (Paulo Lacerda)

"Excellent! The "Wound scars" is still a very serious problem for many people. Many, inclusive, getting to the point of taking their own life. Like you, I have also suffered many losses and marked deceptions. The secret is to be calm and maintain an overall understanding. There is no point in lamenting or thinking about the tragedies, for that only damages us. We need to live life and benefit from the happy moments which are rare. By doing that, everything becomes lighter and then we will find the meaning of life: To help in the evolution of the planet and our own. Very well, my brothers, I wish from the bottom of my heart that you will find the happiness, the success and the realization of your dreams. Be sure, you have in me a friend at any time. My love and my spirit will protect you wherever you are. I believe! (The son of God)

"Thank you. I truly reciprocate. (Paulo Lacerda)

"We will continue our mutual exchange. (Emanuel)

"We have reached the end of this stage. Congratulations everyone! (Messias)

"Amen! (Tadeu Barbosa)

"Let's enjoy the rest of the evening as if it were the last one. Tomorrow, everyone is free to return to their homes and proceed with their path. Everything will be alright. (The seer)

As a respected chief, everyone obeyed his command. They still have time for admiring the stars, continue the small talk about other matters, entertain themselves and pray together. At the end of the evening, they go to sleep. The proposed matter at the start of the adventure was solved and now they can go back to their routine.

The return homes.

The last night spent at the park unfolded in the same way as the previous ones. Quickly dawn arrived and soon daytime. Very early, they wake up, dismantle the tent, keep their belongings and made their way back. They reach the car, get in and leave towards the municipality.

When they arrived, each one would follow different paths. Emanuel and Messias would go to Jeritacó, Aldivan to some place in the backwoods of Pernambuco, Paulo to Catimbau and Tadeu to Buíque. These were the legendary five who had the courage to test their intimacy, their problems and their fears with the readers. That they may value that and take the story as a lesson of life for themselves.

"The world needs men with courage, strength and faith to ask pertinent questions for the benefit of the wellbeing of everybody such as an example, Tadeu's "Wound scars"

The End.

www.ingramcontent.com/pod-product-compliance
Lightning Source LLC
LaVergne TN
LVHW020437080526
838202LV00055B/5235